PUFFIN BOOKS

CHARLIE AND THE CHOCOLATE FACTORY: A PLAY

Who wouldn't want to join Charlie in his Chocolate Factory? Now is your chance. In this dramatization of *Charlie and the Chocolate Factory* you can take it in turns to play all the different parts. You can be Augustus Gloop, Violet Beauregarde, Veruca Salt, Grandpa George or Grandma Georgina, Willy Wonka or even Charlie himself. You can act out Charlie's visit to the chocolate factory and help him test the chocolate. You can create the Great Glass Elevator and the Chocolate River for yourselves. Best of all, you can imagine yourselves helping Willy Wonka test his latest and greatest invention – the chocolate producing television.

You and your class can put your dreams into practice by putting on a performance of this play. It has already been tried by some schools and, with a little simple scenery, you can amuse yourselves and entertain an audience.

Other Roald Dahl/Richard George plays available in Puffins are *James and the Giant Peach*, and *Charlie and the Great Glass Elevator*. *Fantastic Mr Fox* is adapted by Sally Reid.

Other books by Roald Dahl

THE BFG

BOY: Tales of Childhood

CHARLIE AND THE CHOCOLATE FACTORY

CHARLIE AND THE GREAT GLASS ELEVATOR

CHARLIE AND THE GREAT GLASS ELEVATOR:
A Play

THE COMPLETE ADVENTURES OF CHARLIE
AND MR WILLY WONKA

DANNY THE CHAMPION OF THE WORLD

FANTASTIC MR FOX

FANTASTIC MR FOX: A Play

GEORGE'S MARVELLOUS MEDICINE

GOING SOLO

JAMES AND THE GIANT PEACH

JAMES AND THE GIANT PEACH: A Play

THE MAGIC FINGER

MATILDA

THE TWITS

THE WITCHES

DIRTY BEASTS (Picture Book)

THE ENORMOUS CROCODILE (Picture Book)

THE GIRAFFE AND THE PELLY AND ME
(Picture Book)

REVOLTING RHYMES (Picture Book)

THE WONDERFUL STORY OF HENRY SUGAR
AND SIX MORE (for older readers)

ROALD DAHL'S

CHARLIE AND THE CHOCOLATE FACTORY: *A PLAY*

Adapted by Richard R. George
Introduction by Roald Dahl

PUFFIN BOOKS

PUFFIN BOOKS

Published by the Penguin Group
Penguin Books Ltd, 27 Wrights Lane, London W8 5TZ, England
Penguin Books USA Inc., 375 Hudson Street, New York, New York 10014, USA
Penguin Books Australia Ltd, Ringwood, Victoria, Australia
Penguin Books Canada Ltd, 10 Alcorn Avenue, Toronto, Ontario, Canada M4V 3B2
Penguin Books (NZ) Ltd, 182–190 Wairau Road, Auckland 10, New Zealand

Penguin Books Ltd, Registered Offices: Harmondsworth, Middlesex, England

First published by Alfred A. Knopf, Inc., New York, and simultaneously
by Random House of Canada Ltd, Toronto, 1976
Published in Puffin Books 1979
17 19 20 18

Printed in England by Clays Ltd, St Ives plc
Set in Monophoto Baskerville

CONTENTS

This dramatic adaptation of *Charlie and the Chocolate Factory* was presented on 6 June 1973 by Richard R. George and the sixth grade class of Charlotte Cross Elementary School in Lockport, New York.

INTRODUCTION

Early in 1975, I received a letter from Mr Richard R. George, who is a school teacher at Charlotte Cross Elementary School, Lockport, New York. He enclosed a copy of a dramatization he had made of *Charlie and the Chocolate Factory* for his sixth grade students. The play had been put on and it had been 'a smashing success'. In his letter, Mr George wondered whether there was any chance of getting this play published so that other schools and drama groups could have as much fun with it as they had at Charlotte Cross.

I will admit that I was not very keen to read the play. I dreaded having to write back to Mr George, as I have had to do to so many others, telling him that his work was not really suitable for publication. But when I read it, I got a lovely shock. It was awfully good.

I wrote to my publishers in New York, suggesting they read it at once. They did so. They were as enthusiastic as I was. And that, very briefly, is how this play came to be published.

You may ask why I didn't do the dramatization myself. The answer is simply that sometimes I have been too busy and at other times I have been too idle. And anyway, I couldn't possibly have done as skilful a job as Mr George. He knows the limitations and problems of producing a school play far better than I do, and he has used this knowledge superbly. I do hope lots of teachers and children get pleasure and fun out of having a go with this play.

ROALD DAHL

CHARLIE AND THE
CHOCOLATE FACTORY

CAST OF CHARACTERS
(In order of appearance)

Narrator
Augustus Gloop
Veruca Salt
Violet Beauregarde
Mike Teavee
Mr Bucket
Grandma Josephine
Grandpa George
Grandma Georgina
Mrs Bucket
Grandpa Joe
Charlie Bucket
Mrs Gloop
Willy Wonka
Mrs Teavee
Mr Salt
Mrs Salt
Mrs Beauregarde
Mr Teavee
Oompa-Loompas (Offstage, if necessary)

SYNOPSIS OF SCENES

SCENE I

NARRATOR *enters in front of curtain.*

NARRATOR: Welcome to the tale of a delicious adventure in a wonderful land. You can tell it will be delicious – can't you smell it already? [*Sniffs*] Oh, how I love that gorgeous smell! You've all heard of Cadbury's, Rowntree, Fry's, Nestlés, Wonka – what's that? You say, what's Wonka? You mean you *don't* know what Wonka is? Why . . . Wonka Chocolate . . . of course! I admit that Willy Wonka's Chocolate is fairly new but it's also the greatest chocolate ever invented. Why, Willy Wonka himself is the most amazing, the most fantastic, the most extraordinary chocolate maker the world has ever seen. He's invented things like . . . say . . . why . . . I'm not going to *tell* you what he's invented. You came to see for yourself! So I'll let you do just that. But before I do, I should perhaps fill you in on what's been happening around here lately. Because Mr Willy Wonka makes the best chocolate in the whole wide world, three other great chocolate makers known as Mr Fickelgruber, Mr Prodnose, and Mr Slugworth sent spies to work for Mr Wonka in order to discover his secrets. Well, they must have been good spies because soon afterwards, these three chocolate makers began making such delicious Wonka favourites as ice cream that never melts, chewing gum that never loses its flavour, and candy balloons that you could blow up to huge sizes before you popped them with a pin and gobbled them up. Mr Wonka didn't know what to do. He didn't know who the spies were, and if he continued to operate his factory *all* his secrets might be stolen. So he did the only thing he could; he sent all the workers home and closed the factory. You might think that that would be the end of Mr Willy Wonka but no sireee – not him. After months and months went by, the factory suddenly began operating again. But nobody knew who was running the place. Nobody *ever* went *in* and nobody *ever* came *out*. The only thing anyone could see were shadows dancing around in front of the lighted windows . . . mighty strange . . . Well anyway, to get back to the story, soon there was a big article in the town paper saying that Mr Willy Wonka, in order to sell a lot of candy once again, was running a contest. Yes sir, that's right . . . a contest! He had secretly wrapped a Golden Ticket under ordinary wrapping paper in five ordinary candy bars. The candy bars were said to be found anywhere . . . in any shop . . . in any street . . . in any town . . . in any country in the world, upon any counter where Wonka's candies are sold. The five winners will tour Mr Wonka's new factory and take home enough chocolate for the rest of their lives. Now *that*, my friends, is where our story begins. Four of the tickets have already been found. Oh, by the way, would you like to meet the four lucky people? All right, listen and watch carefully! I think they're here somewhere. [*Looks out over audience*] Let's see . . . *Augustus Gloop!* Where are you, Augustus Gloop?

AUGUSTUS GLOOP [*From somewhere in audience*]: Chocolate . . . chocolate . . . *chocolate* . . . CHOCOLATE!!! I . . . LOVE . . . CHOCOLATE! Ummmmmmmmmmmmmmmmmmmmmm . . . food . . . FOOD! [*Smacks lips repeatedly*] *Ummmmmmmmmmmmmmmmmmmmmmmmmmmmmmmmm* . . . I MUST EAT ALL THE TIME . . . *Ummmmmmmmmmmmmm* . . . CHOCOLATE! This Golden Ticket is my meal ticket to . . . uh . . . eat . . . and eat . . . and *eat* . . . and EAT!!! Ummmmmmmmmmmm . . . CHOCOLATE . . . *chocolate* . . . chocolate . . .

NARRATOR: Well, uh, friends, that was our first Golden Ticket finder – Augustus Gloop. Let's see now if the lucky girl who found our second Golden Ticket is here. Oh Violet . . . *Violet Beauregarde?*

VIOLET BEAUREGARDE [*Chewing ferociously on gum, waving arms excitedly, talking in a rapid and loud manner, from somewhere in audience*]: I'm a gumchewer normally, but when I heard about these ticket things of Mr Wonka's, I laid off the gum and switched to candy bars in the hope of striking it lucky. *Now*, of course, I'm right back on gum. I just *adore* gum. I can't do without it. I munch it all day long except for a few minutes at mealtimes when I take it out and stick it behind my ear for safe-keeping. To tell you the honest truth, I simply wouldn't feel *comfortable* if I didn't have that little wedge of gum to chew on every moment of the day, I really wouldn't. My mother says it's not ladylike and it looks ugly to see a girl's jaws going up and down like mine do all the time, but I don't agree. And who's she to criticize, anyway, because if you ask me, I'd say that *her* jaws are going up and down almost as much as mine are just from *yelling* at me every minute of the day. And now, it may interest you to know that this piece of gum I'm chewing right at this moment is one I've been working on for over *three months solid*. That's a record, that is. It's beaten the record held by my best friend, Miss Cornelia Prinzmetel. And was she ever mad! It's my most treasured possession now, this piece of gum is. At nights, I just stick it on the end of the bedpost, and it's as good as ever in the mornings ... a ... bit ... hard ... at ... first ... maybe ...

NARRATOR: Such a, uh, lucky, uh, girl. Isn't she, uh, uh, wonderful? The third Golden Ticket was found by another lucky girl. Her name is Veruca Salt. Is *Veruca here now*?

VERUCA SALT [*From somewhere in audience*]: Where's my Golden Ticket? I want my Golden Ticket! Oh yes . . . *here* it is! As soon as I told my father that I simply *had* to have one of those Golden Tickets, he went out into the town and started buying up all the Wonka candy bars he could lay his hands on. *Thousands* of them, he must have bought. *Hundreds* of thousands! Then he had them loaded on to trucks and sent directly to his own factory. He's in the peanut business, you see, and he's got about a hundred women working for him over at his joint, shelling peanuts for roasting and salting. That's what they do all day long, those women . . . they just sit there shelling peanuts. So he says to them, 'Okay, girls,' he says, 'from now on, you can stop shelling peanuts and start shelling the wrappers off these crazy candy bars instead!' And they did. He had every worker in the place yanking the paper off those bars of chocolate, full speed ahead, from morning 'til night. But three days went by, and we had no luck. Oh . . . it was terrible! I got more and more upset each day, and every time he came home I would scream at him, 'Where's my Golden Ticket! I want my Golden Ticket!' And I would lie for hours on the floor, kicking and yelling in the most disturbing way. Then suddenly, on the evening of the fourth day, one of his women workers yelled, 'I've got it! A Golden Ticket!' And my father said, 'Give it to me, quick!' And she did. And he rushed it home and gave it to me, and now . . . I'm all smiles . . . and we have a happy home . . . once again.

NARRATOR: Thank you, Veruca. Isn't she a lovely girl? Now the fourth and last ticket was found by a boy named Mike Teavee. I wonder if Mike's got his ticket with him? *Where are you, Mike?*

MIKE TEAVEE [*From somewhere in audience*]: Of course I've got a Golden Ticket, but why can't everyone leave me alone? I want to watch television!!! [*He pulls out his guns and fires into the air*] I watch all of the shows every day, even the crummy ones where there's no shooting. I like the gangsters best. They're terrific, those gangsters! Especially when they start pumping each other full of lead . . . or flashing the old stilettos . . . or giving each other the one-two-three, with their knuckledusters! Oh boy, what wouldn't I give to be doing that myself! It's the *life*, I tell you. It's terrific!

NARRATOR: And that folks is, uh, Mike Teavee. Sorry for, uh, bothering you, Mike.

End of Scene 1

SCENE 2

NARRATOR *enters in front of curtain.*

NARRATOR: Now we're going to take a look at the hero of our story, Charlie Bucket, and his family. Let me introduce them to you. [*Curtain opens on Bucket home, a bare room with one chair and a bed. Characters are frozen in place: the four* GRANDPARENTS *in the bed;* MR BUCKET *in chair, reading a newspaper,* CHARLIE, *and* MRS BUCKET *on other side of room*] This is the home of Charlie Bucket. Seven people live here. There are only two rooms and only one bed, so you can see that life is extremely uncomfortable. [*Walks over to the bed*] These two very old people are the father and mother of Mr Bucket. Their names are Grandpa Joe and Grandma Josephine. And these two very old people are the father and mother of Mrs Bucket. Their names are Grandpa George and Grandma Georgina. The bed was given to the four old grandparents because they were so old and tired – and of course they're all over ninety years old. [*Goes to* MR BUCKET] This is Mr Bucket. This is Mrs Bucket. They and little Charlie Bucket sleep in the other room, upon mattresses on the floor. As you know, this can be very cold in the wintertime. They can't buy a better house because they don't have any money and there aren't any better jobs. Mr Bucket is the only one that can work and, well, he lost his job a few weeks ago. Yes, it's very sad, but you see, the toothpaste factory *had* to close down. Without Mr Willy Wonka's Chocolate Factory open, nobody ever got cavities any more and they didn't buy any toothpaste and . . . well, you know how it goes. Oh wait . . . gee, I almost forgot . . . this is our hero – Charlie Bucket. Charlie's a nice boy. Of course he's been starving lately. In fact the whole family has. I'm worried about Charlie, though. Why, did you know that Charlie is so weak from not eating that he walks slowly instead of running like the other kids, so he can save his energy? Well, I've said far too much already. Let's find out what's happening at the Bucket house now . . . uhh, I'll see you later.

[NARRATOR *exits.* BUCKET FAMILY *comes to life*]

MR BUCKET: Well, I see that four children have found Golden Tickets. I wonder who the fifth lucky person will be?

GRANDMA JOSEPHINE: I hope it's no one like that repulsive Gloop boy!

GRANDPA GEORGE: Or as spoiled as that Veruca Salt girl!

GRANDMA GEORGINA: Or as beastly as that bubble-popping Violet Beauregarde!

MRS BUCKET: Or living such a useless life as that Teavee boy!

MR BUCKET [*Looking up from his paper*]: It makes you wonder if all children behave like this nowadays ... like these brats we've been hearing about.

GRANDPA JOE: Of course not! Some do, of course. In fact, quite a lot of them do. But not all.

MRS BUCKET: And now there's only one ticket left.

GRANDMA JOSEPHINE: Quite so ... and just as sure as I'll be having cabbage soup for supper tomorrow, that ticket'll go to some nasty little beast who doesn't deserve it!

GRANDPA JOE: I bet I know somebody who'd like to find that Golden Ticket. How about it, Charlie? You love chocolate more than anyone I ever saw!

CHARLIE: Yes, I sure would, Grandpa Joe! You know ... it just about makes me faint when I have to pass Mr Wonka's Chocolate Factory every day as I go to school. The smell of that wonderful chocolate makes me so dreamy that I often fall asleep and bump into Mr Wonka's fence. But I guess I should realize that dreams don't come true. Just imagine! Me imagining that I could win the fifth

Golden Ticket. Why, it's ... it's ... it's pure imagination.

GRANDPA JOE: Well my boy, it may be pure imagination, but I've heard tell that what you imagine sometimes comes true.

CHARLIE: Gee, you really think so, Grandpa Joe? Gee ... I wonder ...

End of Scene 2

SCENE 3

Bucket home, several days later. GRANDPARENTS, MR *and* MRS BUCKET, *as before.*

MR BUCKET: You know, it sure would have been nice if Charlie had won that fifth Golden Ticket.

MRS BUCKET: You mean with that 10p we gave him for his birthday present yesterday?

MR BUCKET: Yes, the one we gave him to buy the one piece of candy he gets every year.

GRANDMA GEORGINA: And just think how long it took you two to save that 10p.

GRANDPA GEORGE: Yes, now that was really a shame.

GRANDMA JOSEPHINE: But think of how Charlie enjoyed the candy. He just loves Willy Wonka chocolate.

MRS BUCKET: He didn't really *act* that disappointed.

MR BUCKET: No, he didn't –

GRANDPA JOE: Well, he might not have acted disappointed, but that's because he's a fine boy and wouldn't want any of us to feel sorry for him. Why – what boy wouldn't be disappointed? I sure wish he'd won. I'd do anything for that boy. Why, I'd even –

CHARLIE [*Running in excitedly*]: Mum! Dad! Grandpa Joe! Grandfolks! You'll never believe it! You'll never believe what happened!

MRS BUCKET: Good gracious, Charlie – what happened?

CHARLIE: Well . . . I was walking home . . . and the wind was so cold . . . and the snow was blowing so hard . . . and I couldn't see where I was going . . . and I was looking down to protect my face . . . and . . . and –

MR BUCKET [*Excitedly*]: Go on, Charlie . . . go on, Charlie . . . what is it?

CHARLIE: And there it was . . . just lying there in the snow . . . kind of buried . . . and I looked around . . . and no one seemed to look as if they had lost anything . . . and . . . and . . . and so I picked it up and wiped it off . . . and I couldn't believe my eyes –

ALL [*Except* CHARLIE] [*Shouting and screaming*]: You found the Golden Ticket! Charlie found the Golden Ticket! Hurray! Hurray! He did it! He did it!

CHARLIE: No . . . no . . . I . . . I found a 50p piece. [*Everybody looks let down and sad*] But, but, but . . . then I thought it wouldn't hurt if I bought a Wonka Whipple-Scrumptious Fudgemallow Delight since it was . . . my 50 pence . . . and I was just *sooo* hungry for one.

ALL [*Getting excited again*]: Yes . . . yes . . . go on . . . go on.

CHARLIE: Well . . . I took off the wrapper slowly . . . and –

ALL [*Shouting and screaming*]: YOU FOUND THE GOLDEN TICKET! Charlie found the Golden Ticket! Hurray! Hurray! He did it! He did it!

CHARLIE: No . . . no . . . no . . . I ate the candy. There wasn't any Golden Ticket. [*Everybody groans and sighs, acting very sad again*] But then . . . I still had 45 pence left and . . . well . . . you know how I love chocolate –

MRS BUCKET: Oh Charlie, you're not sick are you? You didn't spend all of the money on –

CHARLIE: Well no, as a matter of fact . . . I bought another Whipple-Scrumptious Fudgemallow Delight . . . and . . . and . . . and I FOUND THE FIFTH GOLDEN TICKET!!!

ALL: You *what*?

CHARLIE: I did! I did! I really did! I found the fifth Golden Ticket!!

ALL [*Everyone yelling and dancing around*]: Hurray! Hurray! Hurray! *Yippppppeeeeeeeeeee!* It's off to the chocolate factory!!!

End of Scene 3

SCENE 4

In front of the Chocolate Factory. CHARLIE *and* GRANDPA JOE *enter together as scene opens.*

CHARLIE: Boy, Grandpa Joe, I sure am glad that Dad let you take me today.

GRANDPA JOE: Well, Charlie, I guess he just feels that we understand each other.

CHARLIE: Plus, you seem to know all about Willy Wonka and what's happened to him.

GRANDPA JOE: Well, he's been an important man in this town for a good long time. A lot of people said some unkind things about him after he closed down the factory, but I always felt that he had his reasons. Actually I'm quite excited about this 'Golden Ticket' thing. It's a good excuse to see what *is* going on in that factory and how he's running it.

CHARLIE: Speaking of the Golden Ticket, Grandpa Joe, could I read it one more time? I know it sounds silly, but the whole thing seems so magical.

GRANDPA JOE [*Searching his pockets*]: Sure, Charlie . . . let me see if I can find it . . . ah, here it is.

[*He pulls out a small ticket*]

CHARLIE: Let's see now . . . it says, 'Greetings to you, the lucky finder of this Golden Ticket, from Mr Willy Wonka! I shake you warmly by the hand! Tremendous things are in store for you! Many wonderful surprises await you! For now, I do invite you to come to my factory and be my guest for one whole day – you and all others who are lucky enough to find my Golden Tickets. I, Willy Wonka, will conduct you around the factory myself, showing you everything that there is to see, and afterwards, when it is time to leave, you will be escorted home by a procession of large trucks. These trucks, I can promise you, will be loaded with enough delicious eatables to last you and your entire household for many years. If, at any time thereafter, you should run out of supplies, you have only to come back to the factory and show this Golden Ticket, and I shall be happy to refill your cupboard with whatever you want. In this way, you will be able to keep yourself supplied with tasty morsels for the rest of your life. But this is by no means the most exciting thing that will happen on the day of your visit. I am preparing other surprises that are even more marvellous and more fantastic for you and for all my beloved Golden Ticket holders – mystic and marvellous surprises that will entrance, delight, intrigue, astonish, and perplex you beyond measure. In your wildest dreams you could not imagine that such things could happen to you! Just wait and see!

And now, here are your instructions: the day I have chosen for the visit is the first day in the month of February. On this day, and on no other, you must come to the factory gates at ten o'clock sharp in the morning. Don't be late! And you are allowed to bring with you either one or two members of your own family to look after you and to ensure that you don't get into mischief. One more thing – be certain to have this ticket with you, otherwise you will not be admitted. Signed, Willy Wonka.'

GRANDPA JOE: And today is the first of February, and say, Charlie – look, we're here already . . . and I guess everyone else is arriving together.

[AUGUSTUS GLOOP, VIOLET BEAUREGARDE, VERUCA SALT, MIKE TEAVEE, MRS GLOOP, MR *and* MRS TEAVEE, MR *and* MRS SALT, MRS BEAUREGARDE *enter*. WILLY WONKA *enters from opposite side*]

MRS GLOOP: There he is! That's him! It's Willy Wonka!

WILLY WONKA: Welcome! Welcome! Welcome! Hello, everyone! Let's see now. I wonder if I can recognize all of you by the pictures of you in the newspaper. Let's see. [*Pause*] You're Augustus Gloop.

AUGUSTUS GLOOP: Uhhhhh . . . y-e-a-hhhhh and this is . . . uhh . . . my mother.

WILLY WONKA: Delighted to meet you both! Delighted! Delighted! [*Turns to* VIOLET] You're Violet Beauregarde.

VIOLET BEAUREGARDE: So what if I am – let's just get on with the whole thing, huh?

WILLY WONKA: And you must be Mrs Beauregarde. Very happy to meet you! Very happy! [*Turns to* VERUCA] I think you are . . . yes . . . you're Veruca Salt. And you must be Mr and Mrs Salt.

VERUCA SALT: Don't shake his hand, Daddy – it's probably all sticky and chocolatey from working in the factory. After all, he *does* only run a silly little factory. He's not important enough for you to bother shaking hands with, anyway!

WILLY WONKA: You're Mike Teavee. Enchanted to meet you! Yes . . . enchanted.

MIKE TEAVEE [*Blasting his guns*]: Come on! I'm missing all my favourite TV shows!

MR *and* MRS TEAVEE: And we're the Teavees. Pleased to meet you.

WILLY WONKA: Overjoyed! Overjoyed! [*Turns to* CHARLIE] And you must be the boy who just found the ticket yesterday. Congratulations! You're . . . Charlie Bucket – aren't you?

CHARLIE: Yes sir, thank you. And this, sir, is my Grandpa Joe.

GRANDPA JOE: Howdy, Mr Wonka. I'm real pleased to meet you!

WILLY WONKA: How do you do, Mr Grandpa Joe. How *do* you do! Well now, is that everybody? Hmm-mmmm ... why ... I guess it is! Good! Now will you please follow me! Our tour is about to begin! But *do* keep together! Please don't wander off by yourselves! I shouldn't like to lose any of you at this stage of the proceedings! Oh, dear me, no! Here we are! Through this big red door, please. That's right! It's nice and warm inside! I have to keep it warm inside the factory because of the workers! My workers are used to an extremely hot climate! They can't stand the cold! They'd perish if they went outdoors in this weather! Why, they'd freeze to death!

AUGUSTUS GLOOP: But ... who ... are these ... uhh ... workers?

WILLY WONKA: All in good time, my dear boy! Be patient! You shall see everything as we go along! [*All exit with* WILLY WONKA *remaining alone*] Are all of you inside? Good! Would you mind closing the door? Thank you!
     [*Exit*]

End of Scene 4

The Chocolate Room. The Chocolate River runs across the stage, surrounded by trees and pipes. All enter as scene opens.

AUGUSTUS GLOOP: I'm tired! It seems like we've been turning left, turning right, turning left, and turning right again for a whole hour or so. When are we going to eat? I'm hungry! I want to eat right now! Do you all hear me? *Now*!!

CHARLIE: Did you notice that we've been going downward for the longest time, Grandpa Joe?

GRANDPA JOE: Yes, Charlie, I think I heard Mr Wonka say that we were going underground and that all the most important rooms in his factory are deep down below the surface.

CHARLIE: I wonder why?

GRANDPA JOE: Well, I think he said that there wouldn't be nearly enough space for them up on top. He said that the rooms we are going to see are enormous. *Some* are supposed to be larger than football fields!

WILLY WONKA: Here we are everybody! This is the Chocolate Room. This room is the nerve centre of the whole factory. It's the heart of my whole operation!

AUGUSTUS GLOOP: Uhh ... I don't see anything but that old river over there. Where's the food? I'm hungry!

MRS GLOOP: And just look at those enormous pipes over there. There must be ten or eleven of them. I wonder what they're for?

CHARLIE: Gee, Mr Wonka, what's wrong with your river? It's all brown and muddy-looking.

WILLY WONKA: *Nothing* wrong with it, my boy! *Nothing!* Nothing at all! It's all chocolate! Every drop of that river is hot melted chocolate of the finest quality. The *very finest* quality. There's enough chocolate in there to fill every bathtub in the entire country! *And* all the swimming pools as well! Isn't it *terrific*? And just look at my pipes! They suck up the chocolate and carry it away to all the other rooms in the factory where it is needed! Thousands of gallons an hour, my dear children! Thousands and thousands of gallons!

VERUCA SALT [*Screaming as she looks over the edge of the river*]: Look! Look over there! What is it? He's moving! He's walking! Why, it's a little person! It's a little man! Down there behind one of the pipes!

[*Everyone rushes to the edge of the river to get a better look*]

CHARLIE: She's right, Grandpa! It *is* a little man! Can you see him?

GRANDPA JOE: I see him, Charlie!
[*All now shout in turn*]

MRS GLOOP: There's two of them!

MR SALT: My gosh, so there is!

MRS BEAUREGARDE: There's more than two! There's four or five!

MR TEAVEE: What are they doing?

MRS GLOOP: Where do they come from?

VIOLET BEAUREGARDE: Who are they?

CHARLIE: Aren't they fantastic?

GRANDPA JOE: No higher than my knee!

CHARLIE: Look at their funny long hair! They can't be *real* people!

WILLY WONKA: Nonsense! Of course they are real people! They are some of my workers!

MIKE TEAVEE: That's impossible! There are no people in the world as small as that!

WILLY WONKA: No people in the world as small as that? Then let me tell you something. There are more than three thousand of them in my factory! They are Oompa-Loompas!

CHARLIE: Oompa-Loompas! What do you mean?

WILLY WONKA: Imported direct from Loompaland. And oh, what a terrible country it is! Nothing but thick jungles infested by the most dangerous beasts in the world – hornswogglers and snozzwangers and those terrible wicked whangdoodles. A whangdoodle would eat ten Oompa-Loompas for breakfast and come galloping back for a second helping. When I went out there, I found the little Oompa-Loompas living in tree-houses. They *had* to live in tree-houses to escape from the whangdoodles and the horn-swogglers and the snozzwangers. When I found them they were practically starving to death. They were living on green caterpillars, red beetles, eucalyptus leaves, and the bark of the bong-bong tree. They loved cacao beans too, but only found about one or two a year. They used to dream about cacao beans all night and talk about them all day. It just so happens that the cacao bean is the thing from which all chocolate is made. I myself use billions of cacao beans every week in this factory. So I talked to the leader of the tribe in Oompa-Loompish and told him that his people could have all the cacao beans they wanted if they would just come and work for me and live in my factory. Well, the leader was so happy that he leaped up in the air and threw his bowl of mashed caterpillars right out of his tree-house window. So, here they are! They're wonderful workers. They all speak English now. They love dancing and music. They are always making up songs. I expect you will hear a good deal of singing today from time to time.

VERUCA SALT: Mummy! Daddy! I want an Oompa-Loompa! I want you to get me an Oompa-Loompa! I want an Oompa-Loompa right away! I want to take it home with me! Go on, Daddy! Get . . . me . . . an . . . Oompa-Loompa!

MRS SALT [*Mildly*]: Now, now, my pet. We mustn't interrupt Mr Wonka.

VERUCA SALT [*Screaming*]: But I want an Oompa-Loompa!!!

MR SALT: All right, Veruca, all right. But I can't get it for you this second, sweetie. Please be patient. I'll see that you have one before the day is out.

[AUGUSTUS GLOOP *leans over river*]

MRS GLOOP: Augustus! Augustus, sweetheart! I don't think you had better do that.

WILLY WONKA: Oh, no! Please, Augustus, p-l-e-a-s-e! I beg of you not to do that. My chocolate must be untouched by human hands!

MRS GLOOP: Augustus! Didn't you hear what the man said? Come away from that river at once!

AUGUSTUS GLOOP [*Leaning over further*]: This stuff is *teee-rrific*! Oh boy, I need a bucket to drink it properly!

WILLY WONKA: Augustus ... you *must* come away! *You are dirtying my chocolate!*

MRS GLOOP: Augustus! You'll be giving that nasty cold of yours to about a million people all over the country! Be careful Augustus! You're leaning *too far out*!!
　　[AUGUSTUS *shrieks as he falls in*]

MRS GLOOP: Save him! He'll drown! He can't swim a yard! Save him! Save him!

AUGUSTUS GLOOP: Help! Help! Fish me out!

MRS GLOOP [*To everybody*]: Don't just stand there! *Do* something!

VERUCA SALT: Look! He's being sucked closer to one of the pipes!

MIKE TEAVEE: There he goes!

MRS GLOOP: Oh, help! Murder! Police! Augustus! Come back at once! Where are you going? [*Pause*] He's disappeared. He's *disappeared*! Where does that pipe go to? Quick! Call the fire brigade!

WILLY WONKA: Keep calm. He'll come out of it just fine, you wait and see.

MRS GLOOP: But he'll be turned into marshmallows!

WILLY WONKA: Impossible!

MRS GLOOP: And why *not*, may I ask?

WILLY WONKA: Because that pipe doesn't go anywhere near the Marshmallow Room. It leads to the
room where I make a most delicious kind of
strawberry-flavoured chocolate-coated fudge.

MRS GLOOP: Oh, my poor Augustus! They'll be selling him by the pound all over the country tomorrow morning! [WILLY WONKA *is laughing and*
MRS GLOOP *begins to chase him, trying to hit him with
her purse*] How *dare* you laugh like that when my
boy's just gone up the pipe! You monster! You
think it's a joke, do you? You think that sucking my
boy up into your Fudge Room like that is just one
great colossal joke?

WILLY WONKA: He'll be perfectly safe.

MRS GLOOP: He'll be chocolate fudge!

WILLY WONKA: Never! I wouldn't allow it!

MRS GLOOP: And why not?

WILLY WONKA: Because the taste would be *terrible*!
Just imagine it! Augustus-flavoured chocolate-
coated Gloop! No one would buy it.

MRS GLOOP: I don't want to *think* about it!

WILLY WONKA: Nor do I, and I do promise you,
madam, that your darling boy *is* perfectly safe.

MRS GLOOP: If he's safe, then where is he? Lead me
to him this instant!

WILLY WONKA: Go over to one of the Oompa-
Loompas and ask him to show you to the Fudge
Room. When you get there, take a long stick and
start poking around inside the big chocolate-mixing
barrel. He should be there. Don't leave him in there
too long though, or he's liable to get poured out
into the fudge boiler, and that really would be a
disaster, wouldn't it? My fudge would become
quite uneatable!

MRS GLOOP [*Shrieking*]: What . . . what . . . *what* did
you say?

WILLY WONKA: I'm joking – forgive me. Good-bye,
Mrs Gloop . . . see you later.

> [MRS GLOOP *exits. All others exit in opposite
> direction*]

OOMPA-LOOMPAS:
> Augustus Gloop! Augustus Gloop!
> The great big greedy nincompoop!
> How long could we allow this beast
> To gorge and guzzle, feed and feast
> On everything he wanted to?
> Great Scott! It simply wouldn't do!
> So what we do in cases such
> As this, we use the gentle touch,
> 'Come on!' we cried. 'The time is ripe
> To send him shooting up the pipe!'
> But don't, dear children, be alarmed;
> Augustus Gloop will not be harmed,

Although, of course, we must admit
He will be altered quite a bit.
He'll be quite changed from what he's been,
When he goes through the fudge machine:
Slowly, the wheels go round and round,
The cogs begin to grind and pound;
A hundred knives go slice, slice, slice;
We add some sugar, cream, and spice;
Then out he comes! And now! By grace!
A miracle has taken place!
This boy, who only just before
Was loathed by men from shore to shore,
This greedy brute, this louse's ear,
Is loved by people everywhere!
For who could hate or bear a grudge
Against a luscious bit of fudge?

End of Scene 5

SCENE 6

NARRATOR *enters in front of curtain.*

NARRATOR: Poor Augustus ... well, I bet we've seen the last of him for a while. Now you folks are really in for a treat! Did you know that Willy Wonka had his very own yacht? That's right! His very own! And boy, is it sharp! It's bright pink and has about ten Oompa-Loompas inside, pulling all of the oars! Well there's no point telling you all about the boat, because in just a second ... you should ... be able to see it coming ... up the tunnel ... yes ... yes ... *here it comes now!*

> [NARRATOR *exits. Curtain opens to Chocolate River, now stage front. There are three doors behind the river which say 'Cream Room', 'Whip Room', and 'Bean Room'. Boat with visitors enters as scene opens*]

VIOLET BEAUREGARDE: It sure is dark in here! How can these dumb Oompa-Loompas see where they're going?

WILLY WONKA [*Hooting with laughter*]: There's no knowing where they're going!

There's no earthly way of knowing
Which direction they are going!
There's no knowing where they're rowing,
Or which way the river's flowing!
Not a speck of light is showing,
So the danger must be growing,
For the rowers keep on rowing,
And they're certainly not showing
Any signs that they are slowing . . .

MRS SALT: He's gone off his rocker!

ALL: He's crazy!

MIKE TEAVEE: He's balmy!

VERUCA SALT: He's nutty!

VIOLET BEAUREGARDE: He's screwy!

MRS BEAUREGARDE: He's batty!

MRS TEAVEE: He's dippy!

MR SALT: He's dotty!

MIKE TEAVEE: He's daffy!

VERUCA SALT: He's goofy!

VIOLET BEAUREGARDE: He's buggy!

MRS BEAUREGARDE: He's wacky!

MR TEAVEE: He's loony!

GRANDPA JOE: Oh, no he's not!

WILLY WONKA: Switch on the lights! Row faster! Faster!

[*The boat moves along*]

CHARLIE: Look, Grandpa! There's a door in the wall! It says ... Cream Room – dairy cream, whipped cream, violet cream, coffee cream, pineapple cream, vanilla cream, and ... hair cream?

MIKE TEAVEE: Hair cream? You don't eat *hair cream*!

WILLY WONKA: Row on! There's no time to answer silly questions!

[*The boat moves along*]

CHARLIE: Look ... another door! Whip Room!

VERUCA SALT: Whips? What on earth do you use whips for?

WILLY WONKA: For whipping cream, of course! How can you whip cream without whips? Whipped cream isn't whipped cream at all, unless it's been whipped with whips – just as a poached egg isn't a poached egg unless it's been stolen from the woods in the dead of night! Row on, please!

[*The boat moves along*]

CHARLIE: Bean Room! Cacao beans, coffee beans, jelly beans, and Has Beans.

VIOLET BEAUREGARDE: Has Beans?

WILLY WONKA: You're one yourself! No time for arguing! Press on! Press on! [*Pause*] Stop the boat! We're *there*!

MIKE TEAVEE: We're where?

WILLY WONKA: Up there!

MIKE TEAVEE: What's up there?

WILLY WONKA: You'll see.

End of Scene 6

SCENE 7

The Invention Room. It is filled with stoves and pipes, pots and kettles, and many strange machines. All enter as scene opens.

WILLY WONKA: This is the most important room in the entire factory! All my most secret new inventions are cooking and simmering in here! Old Fickelgruber would give his front teeth to be allowed inside, just for three minutes! So would Prodnose and Slugworth and all the other rotten chocolate makers! But now, listen to me! I want no messing about when you go in! No touching! No meddling! And *no tasting*! Is that agreed?

ALL CHILDREN: Yes, yes! We won't touch a thing!
 [*Everyone looks around in amazement.* WILLY WONKA *runs around and jumps in excitement from place to place. He approaches and gazes into a machine*]

WILLY WONKA: Everlasting Gobstoppers! They're completely new! I am inventing them for children who are given very little pocket money. You can put an Everlasting Gobstopper in your mouth and you can suck it and suck it and suck it and suck it and suck it and . . . it will never get any smaller!

VIOLET BEAUREGARDE: It's like gum!

WILLY WONKA: It is *not* like gum! Gum is for chewing, and if you tried chewing one of these Gobstoppers here, you'd break your teeth off. But they *taste* terrific! And they change colour once a week! Now that machine over there makes hair toffee but it's not quite perfected yet. But I'll get the mixture right soon! And when I do, then there'll be no excuse any more for little boys and girls going about with bald heads!

MIKE TEAVEE: But Mr Wonka, little boys and girls never go about with –

WILLY WONKA: Don't argue, my dear child . . . *please* don't argue! Now over here, if you will all step this way, I will show you something I am *terrifically* proud of. Oh, do be careful! Stand back!
  [*He stops at centre stage in front of the Great Gum Machine*]

WILLY WONKA: Here we go!
  [*He begins pushing buttons, and all kinds of noises and lights occur. Finally a small strip of grey cardboard appears from side of machine*]

MIKE TEAVEE: You mean that's *all*?

WILLY WONKA [*Proudly*]: That's all! Don't you know what it is?

VIOLET BEAUREGARDE [*Yelling*]: By gum, it's *gum*!!! It's a stick of chewing gum!

WILLY WONKA: Right you are! [*Slapping* VIOLET *hard on the back*] It's a stick of the most amazing and fabulous and sensational gum in the world! This gum is a fantastic gum – in that it's a chewing-gum meal! It's a whole three-course dinner all by itself! When I start selling this gum in the shops, it will change everything. It will be the *end* of cooking, marketing, forks, plates, washing up, and garbage! This piece of gum I've just made happens to be tomato soup, roast beef, *and* blueberry pie! But you can have almost anything you want!

VIOLET BEAUREGARDE: What do you mean by that?

WILLY WONKA: If you were to start chewing it, you would actually taste *all* of those things. *And* it fills you up! It satisfies you! It's terrific!

VERUCA SALT: It's utterly impossible!

VIOLET BEAUREGARDE: Just so long as it's gum, and I can chew it . . . then that's for me! [*She takes her own piece of gum out of her mouth and sticks it behind her left ear*] Come on, Mr Wonka, hand over this magic gum of yours . . . and we'll see if the thing works!

MRS BEAUREGARDE: Now, Violet . . . let's not do anything silly.

VIOLET BEAUREGARDE: I want the gum! What's so silly?

WILLY WONKA: I would rather you didn't take it. You see, I haven't got it quite right yet. There are still one or two things –

VIOLET BEAUREGARDE [*Interrupting*]: Oh, to heck with that!
[*She grabs the gum and pops it into her mouth*]

WILLY WONKA: Don't!

VIOLET BEAUREGARDE: Fabulous! It's great!

WILLY WONKA: Spit it out!

MRS BEAUREGARDE: Keep chewing, kiddo! Keep right on chewing, baby! This is a great day for the Beauregardes! Our little girl is the first person in the world to have a chewing-gum meal!

WILLY WONKA [*Wringing his hands*]: No – no – no – no – no! It isn't ready for eating! It isn't right! You mustn't do it!

MRS BEAUREGARDE: Good heavens, girl! What's happening to your nose? It's turning *blue*!

VIOLET BEAUREGARDE: Oh, be quiet, mother, and let me finish!

MRS BEAUREGARDE: Your cheeks! Your chin! Your whole face is turning *blue*! Mercy save us! The girl's going blue and purple all over! Violet, you're turn-

ing violet, Violet! What *is* happening to you? You're glowing all over! The whole room is glowing!
[*Blue lights on only*]

WILLY WONKA [*Sighing and shaking head sadly*]: I *told* you I hadn't got it quite right. It always goes wrong when we come to the dessert. It's the blueberry pie that does it. But I'll get it right one day, you wait and see!

MRS BEAUREGARDE: Violet . . . you're swelling up!
[VIOLET *begins backing off stage*]

VIOLET BEAUREGARDE: I feel most peculiar!
[VIOLET *now disappears off stage*]

MRS BEAUREGARDE: You're swelling up! You're *blowing up like a balloon*!

WILLY WONKA: Like a *blueberry*!

MRS BEAUREGARDE: Call a doctor!

MR SALT: Prick her with a pin!

MRS BEAUREGARDE [*Wringing her hands helplessly*]: Save her!

WILLY WONKA: It always happens like this. All the Oompa-Loompas that tried it finished up as blueberries. It's *most* annoying. I just *can't* understand it.

MRS BEAUREGARDE: But I don't *want* a blueberry for a daughter! Put her back this instant!

WILLY WONKA: Tell the Oompa-Loompas over there to roll Miss Beauregarde into the Juicing Room at once!

MRS BEAUREGARDE: The *Juicing Room*? What for?

WILLY WONKA: To *squeeze* her! We've got to squeeze the juice out of her immediately. After that, we'll just have to see how she comes out. But *don't* worry. We'll get her repaired if it's the *last thing we do*. I *am* sorry about it all ... I really am ...

[MRS BEAUREGARDE *walks off following* VIO-LET]

CHARLIE: Mr Wonka? Will Violet ever be all right again?

WILLY WONKA: She'll come out of the de-juicing machine just as thin as a whistle – and she'll be purple. Purple from head to toe! But there you are! That's what comes from chewing disgusting gum all day long!

MIKE TEAVEE: If it's so *disgusting*, then why do you make it in your factory?

WILLY WONKA: I can't hear a word you're saying. Come on! Off we go! Follow me!

[*All exit*]

OOMPA-LOOMPAS:
Dear friends, we surely all agree
There's almost nothing worse to see

Than some repulsive little bum
Who's always chewing chewing gum.
This sticky habit's bound to send
The chewer to a sticky end.
Did any of you ever know
A person called Miss Bigelow?
This dreadful woman saw no wrong
In chewing, chewing all day long.
And when she couldn't find her gum,
She'd chew up the linoleum,
Or anything that happened near –
A pair of boots, the postman's ear,
Or other people's underclothes,
And once she chewed her boyfriend's nose.
For years and years she chewed away,
Consuming fifty packs a day,
Until one summer's eve, alas,
A horrid business came to pass.
Miss Bigelow went late to bed,
For half an hour she lay and read,
At last, she put her gum away
Upon a special little tray,
And settled back and went to sleep –
(She managed this by counting sheep.)
But now, how strange! Although she
    slept,
Those massive jaws of hers still kept
On chewing, chewing through the night,
Even with nothing there to bite.

This sleeping woman's great big trap
Opening and shutting, snap-snap-snap!
Faster and faster, chop-chop-chop,
The noise went on, it wouldn't stop.
Until at last her jaws decide
To pause and open extra wide,
And with the most tremendous chew
They bit the lady's tongue in two.
And that is why we'll try so hard
To save Miss Violet Beauregarde
From suffering an equal fate.
She's still quite young. It's not too late,
Provided she survives the cure.
We hope she does. We can't be sure.

End of Scene 7

SCENE 8

In front of the Nut Room. At centre stage, facing stage left, is a door with a glass panel; behind it, a pile of nuts and a rubbish chute [inside the room]. All enter as scene opens.

WILLY WONKA: All right, stop here for a moment and catch your breath. And take a peek through the glass panel of this door. But don't go in! Whatever you do, don't go into . . . The Nut Room! If you go in, you'll disturb the miniature squirrels!

CHARLIE [*Peeking through the panel*]: Oh *look*, Grandpa! Look!

VERUCA SALT: Miniature squirrels!

MIKE TEAVEE: Jeepers! There must be a hundred of them around that pile of walnuts over there.

WILLY WONKA: These squirrels are specially trained for getting the nuts out of walnuts.

MIKE TEAVEE: Why use squirrels? Why not use Oompa-Loompas?

WILLY WONKA: Nobody can get walnuts out of walnut shells in one piece, except squirrels. I *insist* on using only *whole* walnuts in my factory – so I use squirrels to do the job. And see how they first tap each walnut with their knuckles – to be sure it's not a bad one! If it's bad, it makes a hollow sound, and they don't bother to open it. They simply throw it down the garbage chute.

VERUCA SALT: Hey Daddy! I've decided I want a squirrel! Get me one of those squirrels!

MR SALT: Don't be silly, sweetheart. These all belong to Mr Wonka.

VERUCA SALT: I don't care about that! I want one! All I've *got* at home is two dogs, and four cats, and six bunny rabbits, and two parakeets, and three canaries, and a green parrot, and a turtle, and a bowl of gold-fish, and a cage of white mice, and a silly old hamster! I . . . want . . . a . . . *squirrel*!!!

MR SALT: All right, my pet, Daddy'll get you a squirrel just as soon as he possibly can.

VERUCA SALT: But I don't want any . . . old . . . squirrel! I want a *trained* squirrel.

MR SALT: Very well. [*Taking out a wallet full of money*] Wonka? How much d'you want for one of these crazy squirrels? Name your price!

WILLY WONKA: They're not for sale. She can't have one.

VERUCA SALT [*Furious*]: Who says I can't?! I'm going in to grab me a squirrel this very minute!

WILLY WONKA: Don't!

> [VERUCA *goes through the door and approaches the squirrel she wants*]

VERUCA SALT: All right, I'll have *you*!

> [*As she reaches out, she acts as if all the squirrels are leaping on to her. She struggles and wriggles and screams*]

WILLY WONKA: No – no – no! They've all jumped on her! All of them! Twenty-five of them have her right arm pinned down. Twenty-five have her left arm pinned down. Twenty-five have her right leg anchored to the ground. Twenty-four have her left leg. And the last squirrel ... it's ... it's climbed up on her shoulders and started tap-tap-tapping on Veruca's head with its knuckles!

MRS SALT: Save her! Veruca! Come back! What are they doing to her?

WILLY WONKA: They're testing her to see if she's a bad nut – watch! [VERUCA *now acts as if she's being dragged across the floor towards the rubbish chute*] My goodness! She is a bad nut after all. Her head must have sounded quite hollow!

> [VERUCA *kicks and screams but to no avail*]

MRS SALT: Where are they taking her?

WILLY WONKA: She's going where all the other bad nuts go – down the rubbish chute!

MR SALT: By golly . . . she *is* going down the chute!

    [VERUCA *wriggles herself into chute and out of sight*]

WILLY WONKA: She's gone!

MRS SALT: Where do you suppose she's gone to?

WILLY WONKA: That particular chute runs directly into the great big main rubbish pipe which carries away all the rubbish from every part of the factory – all the floor sweepings and potato peelings and rotten cabbages and fish heads and stuff like that.

MIKE TEAVEE: Who eats fish and cabbage and potatoes in this factory, I'd like to know?

WILLY WONKA: I do, of course. You don't think I live on cacao beans, do you? And of course, the pipe goes to the furnace in the end.

MR SALT: Now see here, Wonka . . . I think you've gone just a shade too far this time, I do indeed. My daughter may be a bit of a frump – I don't mind admitting it – but that doesn't mean you can roast her to a crisp. I'll have you know I'm extremely cross about this – I really am.

WILLY WONKA: Oh, don't be cross, my dear sir! I expect she'll turn up again sooner or later. She may not even have gone down the pipe at all. She may be stuck in the chute, just below the entrance hole.

And if that's the case, all you'll have to do is go in and pull her up again.

[MRS SALT *runs into the Nut Room and looks into the hole, bending over*]

MRS SALT: Veruca! Are you down there?

[*She leans over further and falls into the chute, as if pushed by the squirrels*]

WILLY WONKA: Oh no! The squirrels have pushed her, too!

MR SALT: Good gracious me! What a lot of rubbish there's going to be today! [*He leans over the hole and peers in*] What's it like down there, Angina? [*Acts as if being pushed by the squirrels too*] Help!

[*He also falls into the chute*]

CHARLIE: Oh dear! What on earth's going to happen to them now?

WILLY WONKA: I expect someone will catch them at the bottom of the chute.

CHARLIE: But what about the great fiery incinerator?

WILLY WONKA: Oh *that*! They only light it every other day. Perhaps this is one of the days when they let it go out. You never know – they might be lucky. I've never seen anything like it! The children are disappearing like rabbits! Oh well, shall we move on?

CHARLIE *and* GRANDPA JOE: Oh, yes!

MIKE TEAVEE: My feet are getting tired! I want to watch television!

WILLY WONKA: If you're tired then we'd better take the elevator. It's just down the hall. Come on!
[*All exit*]

OOMPA-LOOMPAS:
Veruca Salt, the little brute,
Has just gone down the rubbish chute,
(And as we very rightly thought
That in a case like this we ought
To see the thing completely through,
We've polished off her parents, too.)
Down goes Veruca! Down the drain!
And here, perhaps, we should explain
That she will meet, as she descends,
A rather different set of friends:
Some liverwurst so old and grey
One smelled it from a mile away,
A rotten nut, a reeky pear,
A thing the cat left on the stair,
And lots of other things as well,
Each with a rather horrid smell.
These are Veruca's new found friends
That she will meet as she descends,
And this is the price she has to pay
For going so very far astray.
But now, my dears, we think you might
Be wondering – is it really right

That every single bit of blame
And all the scolding and the shame
Should fall upon Veruca Salt?
Is she the only one at fault?
For though she's spoiled, and dreadfully so,
A girl can't spoil herself, you know.
Who turned her into such a brat?
Who are the culprits? Who did that?
Alas! You needn't look so far
To find out who these sinners are.
They are (and this is very sad)
Her loving parents, Mum and Dad.
And that is why we're glad they fell
Into the rubbish chute as well.

End of Scene 8

SCENE 9

By the Great Glass Elevator. Elevator is at centre stage, and all enter and gather around it as scene opens.

CHARLIE: Wow! Look at that! It's a Great Glass Elevator! And look at all the buttons all over.

WILLY WONKA: This isn't just an ordinary up-and-down elevator! This elevator can go sideways and longways and slantways and any other way you can think of! It can visit any single room in the whole factory, no matter where it is! You simply press the button and *zing*! You're off!

GRANDPA JOE: Fantastic!

CHARLIE: *Look!* Each button is labelled!

WILLY WONKA: And each button stands for a room!

MIKE TEAVEE: Yeah . . . let's see. It says, Strawberry-juice Water Pistols, Exploding Candies for your enemies, Stickjaw for talkative parents, Invisible Chocolate Bars for eating in class, Rainbow Drops – suck them and you can spit in six different colours –

WILLY WONKA: Come on! Enough! Enough! We can't wait all day!

    [*They enter the elevator*]

MIKE TEAVEE: Isn't there a *Television* Room in all this lot?

WILLY WONKA: Certainly! Right here!
[*He points to a button*]

MIKE TEAVEE: Whoopee! That's for me!
[*He presses a button and the elevator shakes*]

WILLY WONKA [*Laughing*]: Hang on, everybody!

MR TEAVEE: I'm going to be *sick*!

WILLY WONKA: Please don't be sick.

MR TEAVEE: Try and stop me!

WILLY WONKA [*Holding his hat in front of* MR TEAVEE]: Then you'd better take this!

MR TEAVEE: Make this awful thing stop!

WILLY WONKA: Can't do that! It won't stop 'til we get there. I only hope no one is using the other elevator at this moment.

MIKE TEAVEE: What . . . other . . . elevator?

WILLY WONKA: The one that goes the opposite way on the same track as this one!

MR TEAVEE: Holy mackerel! You mean we might have a collision?

WILLY WONKA: I've always been lucky so far.

MR TEAVEE: Now I *am* going to be sick!

WILLY WONKA: No! No! Not now! We're nearly there! Don't spoil my hat!

[*Elevator stops shaking*]

MIKE TEAVEE: Some . . . ride!

MR TEAVEE: Never again!

WILLY WONKA: Just a minute now! Listen to me! Before we go into this Television-Chocolate Room, I want to warn you. There is dangerous stuff around in here and you *must not* tamper with it! [*Pause*] Okay, everybody out!

[*All leave elevator and exit*]

End of Scene 9

SCENE 10

The Television-Chocolate Testing Room. It is completely bare except for a large television camera at one end, a large television screen at the other, and several bright floodlights. All enter as scene opens.

WILLY WONKA [*Hopping up and down with excitement*]: Here we go! This is the Testing Room for my very latest and greatest invention – *Television Chocolate*!

MIKE TEAVEE: But *what* is Television Chocolate?

WILLY WONKA: Good heavens, child, stop interrupting me! It works by television. I don't like television myself. I suppose it's all right in small doses, but children never seem to be able to take it in small doses. They want to sit there all day long . . . staring and staring at the screen –

MIKE TEAVEE: That's me!

MR TEAVEE. Shut up!

WILLY WONKA: Thank you. Now then! The very first time I saw ordinary television working, I was struck by a tremendous idea. If a photograph could be broken up into millions of pieces, and the pieces sent whizzing through the air until they hit an antenna, and then put together again on a screen – why couldn't I send a *real* bar of chocolate whizzing through the air in tiny pieces, and then put the pieces together at the other end, all ready to be eaten?

MIKE TEAVEE: Impossible!

WILLY WONKA: Think so? Watch me send a bar of chocolate from one end of this room to the other – by television. Bring me that chocolate bar, please. [CHARLIE *brings over an enormous bar of chocolate from off stage*] It has to be big, because whenever you send something by television, it always comes out much smaller than it was when it went in. Here we go then! Get ready! [MIKE *wanders curiously towards the camera*] No! No! Stop! You there! Mike Teavee! Stand back! You're too close! There are dangerous rays coming out of that thing! They could break you up into a million tiny pieces in one second! [MIKE *backs away*] That's better! Now then . . . switch on!
    [*Lights flash and bar disappears through slit in curtain*]

GRANDPA JOE [*Waving his arms and shouting*]: The chocolate's gone!

WILLY WONKA: It's on its way! It's now rushing through the air above our heads in a million tiny pieces. *Quick!* Come over here! [*All dash over to the*

other side of the stage, to TV screen] Watch the screen!
[*Small bar of chocolate appears through slit in curtain and lighted screen*] Take it!

MIKE TEAVEE [*Laughing*]: How *can* you take it? It's just a picture on a television screen!

> [CHARLIE *reaches out and the chocolate miraculously goes into his hands*]

GRANDPA JOE: It's absolutely fantastic! It's . . . it's . . . it's a *miracle*!

WILLY WONKA: Just *imagine* – when I start using this across the country, a commercial will flash on to the screen and a voice will say, 'Eat Wonka's Chocolates! They're the best in the world! If you don't believe us, try one for yourself . . . now!!!!'

GRANDPA JOE: Terrific!

MIKE TEAVEE [*Shouting*]: But Mr Wonka, can you send other things through the air in the same way? Like people? Could you send a real live person from one place to another in the same way?

WILLY WONKA: A person? Are you off your rocker?

MIKE TEAVEE: But *could* it be done?

WILLY WONKA: Good heavens, child. I really don't know . . . I suppose it could . . . yes, I'm pretty sure it could . . . of course it could. I wouldn't like to risk it though – it might have some very nasty results.

[MIKE *is off and moving when he hears* WILLY WONKA *say* '*I'm pretty sure*']

MIKE TEAVEE: Look at me! I'm going to be the first person in the world to be sent by television!

WILLY WONKA: No! No! No! *No!*

MR TEAVEE: Mike! Stop! Come back! You'll be turned into a million tiny pieces!

MIKE TEAVEE: See you later, alligator!
[*He jumps into the glare of the light and then disappears through folds in curtain*]

MR TEAVEE [*Running to spot where* MIKE *disappeared*]: He's gone!

WILLY WONKA [*Placing a hand on* MR TEAVEE'*s shoulder*]: We shall have to hope for the best. We must pray that your little boy will come out unharmed at the other end. We must watch the television screen. He may come through at any moment.
[*Everyone stares at the screen*]

MR TEAVEE [*Wiping his brow nervously*]: He's taking a heck of a long time to come across.

WILLY WONKA: Hold everything! Watch the screen! Something's happening!

MR TEAVEE: Here he comes! Yes, that's him all right!

[*Pause*] But he's a *midget*! Isn't he going to get any bigger?

WILLY WONKA: Grab him! *Quick!* [MR TEAVEE *acts as if he grabs something*] He's *completely* okay!

MR TEAVEE [*Acting as if something is in his hand*]: You call that okay? He's *shrunk*!

WILLY WONKA: Of course he's shrunk. What did you expect?

MR TEAVEE: This is terrible! I can't send him back to school like this! He'll get squashed! He won't be able to do *anything*! [*He acts as if he is listening to* MIKE, *in his hand*] What did you say, Mike? [*Pause*] Never! No, you will *not* be able to watch television! I'm throwing the television set right out the window the moment we get home. I've had *enough* of television! What, Mike? [*Pause*] I don't care what you want . . . or how much you jump and scream! [*He puts him in his pocket, acting as if he is secure there, slapping his pocket*] There!

CHARLIE: Gee, how will Mike ever grow again?

WILLY WONKA [*Stroking his beard thoughtfully*]: Well . . . small boys *are* extremely springy and elastic, so maybe he'll stretch if we put him on a special machine I have for testing the tough stretchiness of chewing gum!

MR TEAVEE: How far do you think he'll stretch?

WILLY WONKA: Maybe *miles*! Anyway, he'll be awfully thin! But we'll fatten him up with all my super vitamin candy. It contains all the vitamins from A to Z! [*Writing instructions on a sheet of paper*] Mr Teavee, just hand these orders to the Oompa-Loompas over there . . . and don't look so worried! They all come out in the wash you know – every one of them.

    [*All exit*]

OOMPA-LOOMPAS:

> The most important thing we've learned,
> So far as children are concerned,
> Is never, never, never let
> Them near your television set –
> They loll and slop and lounge about,
> And stare until their eyes pop out.
> Oh yes, we know it keeps them still,
> They don't climb out the window sill,
> They never fight or kick or punch,
> They leave you free to cook the lunch
> And wash the dishes in the sink –
> But did you ever stop to think,
> To wonder just exactly what
> This does to your beloved tot?
> It rots the senses in the head!
> It kills imagination dead!

His brain becomes as soft as cheese!
His powers of thinking rust and freeze!
He cannot think – he only sees!
'All right!' you'll cry. 'All right!' you'll say,
'But if we take the set away,
What shall we do to entertain
Our darling children? Please explain!'
We'll answer this by asking you,
What used the darling ones to do?
They . . . used . . . to . . . read! They'd read and
    read,
And read and read, and then proceed
To read some more. Great Scott! Gadzooks!
One half their lives was reading books!
Such wondrous, fine, fantastic tales
Of dragons, gypsies, queens, and whales
And pirates wearing purple pants,
And sailing ships and elephants,
And cannibals crouching 'round the pot,
Stirring away at something hot.
Oh, books, what books they used to know,
Those children living long ago!
So please, oh please, we beg, we pray,
Go throw your TV set away,
Fear not, because we promise you
That, in about a week or two
Of having nothing else to do,
They'll now begin to feel the need
Of having something good to read.

P.S. regarding Mike Teavee,
We very much regret that we
Shall simply have to wait and see
If we can get him back his height.
But if we can't – it serves him right.

End of Scene 10

SCENE II

Somewhere in the Chocolate Factory. WILLY WONKA,
CHARLIE *and* GRANDPA JOE *enter as scene opens.*

WILLY WONKA: Which room shall it be next? Hurry
up! We must be going! And how many children are
left now? [*Looks around*] Hmmmmmmmmmmmmm-
mmmm!

GRANDPA JOE: I guess there's only Charlie left now,
Mr Wonka.

WILLY WONKA [*Pretending to be surprised*]: You mean
. . . you're the only one left?

CHARLIE: Why . . . yes.

WILLY WONKA [*Suddenly exploding with excitement*]:
But my dear boy, *that means you've won!* [*He shakes*
CHARLIE'S *hand furiously*] Oh, I do congratulate
you! I really do! I'm absolutely delighted! It
couldn't be better! How wonderful this is! I had a
hunch, you know – right from the beginning – that
it was going to be you! Well done, Charlie . . . well
done! But we mustn't dilly! We mustn't dally! We
have an *enormous* number of things to do before the

day is out! Just think of the *arrangements* that have to be made!

CHARLIE: Wait, Mr Wonka ... I'm afraid I don't understand all of this! What are you talking about?

WILLY WONKA: Oh ... *do* forgive me! I get carried away at times. I forgot that you didn't know –

CHARLIE: Know *what*?

WILLY WONKA [*Becoming quiet and serious*]: You know, Charlie, I love my chocolate factory. [*Pause*] Tell me, Charlie, do you love my chocolate factory? Think carefully, because it's very important – how you feel.

CHARLIE [*Very thoughtfully*]: Well, Mr Wonka, all that I can say is that I've *never* spent a more fantastic day *anywhere* ... in my *whole life*. I've been *very*, *very* happy. Do I love this factory? [*Pause*] Yes ... yes, I think I do! It means ... a great deal to me.

GRANDPA JOE: Why do you ask, Mr Wonka?

WILLY WONKA: Well ... of course Charlie and all of the others will receive all of the candy I promised, but I want *Charlie* to receive *much more*! You see, this whole day has been a *contest*. It's been a contest to find out who would be the best person for the job.

CHARLIE: What job?

WILLY WONKA: Well you see, I'm tired, Charlie. I'm not getting any younger, and it isn't as easy to carry out my ideas as . . . as . . . it once was. I need some help. That means . . . *you*!

CHARLIE: Me?

WILLY WONKA: Yes! I would like you and Grandpa Joe and, of course, all the rest of your family, to move here – and live here – *permanently*! I would like to have someone who will take over . . . after I've gone. I have no family, and I can think of *no one* I would like to run the factory more than *you*. This would be after I've trained you and taught you everything I know, of course! I've watched you all day, and *you* are the type of person that will appreciate this factory . . . and care for it as I have, all these years. Will you accept my offer? If you do, *everything* that I have is yours.

CHARLIE: Will I? *Wow!* This is more than I could have ever imagined! *Will* I? Of course I will, Mr Wonka! Thank you! *Thank you!* Just think of it, Grandpa Joe! Wait until we tell Dad and Mum and the grandfolks! It's going to be *our* chocolate factory! And we're never *ever* going to starve again! Just think of all that chocolate! Oh, just you wait and see!

Curtain

SOME SUGGESTIONS
FOR STAGING

A WORD ABOUT THE PLAY

In adapting *Charlie and the Chocolate Factory* as a play, I have tried to keep the speaking parts and the action as simplified as possible, while still true to Roald Dahl's original story. The following suggestions for characterization, scenery, props, and lighting are based on ideas we used in our own production. As you will see, all the properties are made out of everyday materials (cardboard boxes, chairs, etc.) which are, for the most part, easily obtainable.

The setting for each scene can be as simple or as elaborate as you wish. The play could be performed quite effectively on a bare stage or with only a few small props and signs to indicate the various scenes ('Chocolate Room', 'Nut Room', etc.). Or, if you like, the descriptions at the opening of each scene can be expanded into fuller sets. Playing music before, during, and after the play can also lend an air of 'mood' to the production. It can be quite helpful as a time-filler between scenes, too.

However you choose to put on the show, the important idea is for the cast and crew to use their own imaginations, and then let the audience use theirs as well.

RICHARD R. GEORGE

THE NARRATIONS

The Narrator can be located on the side of the stage or in front of the curtain if there is one. In some auditoriums he can more effectively commentate with the use of a hand microphone. This is particularly helpful during Scene 2, when he actually goes over to each member of the Bucket family in their frozen positions and discusses them.

Augustus Gloop, Violet Beauregarde, Veruca Salt, and Mike Teavee can perform their long speeches in Scene 1 by sitting in prearranged seats in the audience when the play begins. As the Narrator introduces each one in turn, he or she rises and speaks with very slow but obvious movements of the hands, arms and head. You can use a filmstrip projector or spotlight with a fan or flickering hand in front of it if you want to create the effect of a strobe-light.

The Oompa-Loompa narrations can be done on tape through speakers or by a chorus while the scenes are being changed. Some suggestions for creating Oompa-Loompas are given with the scenery and props.

SCENERY AND PROPERTIES

Grandparents' Bed
Take four chairs and place them facing each other,
two by two. Separate the pairs by several feet.

Lay a board across the seats of all four chairs, and
cover the whole thing with a sheet or blankets.

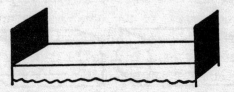

All four grandparents will now be able to sit up in the
crowded bed, facing each other.

Golden Ticket
Charlie should have a very small cardboard ticket
when he reads the information to Grandpa Joe in
Scene 4. The audience should be able to see the ticket,

but he should have the information memorized so that the humour might come through in realizing it would be impossible for so many words to be on such a small ticket.

Chocolate River
Take a couple of large cardboard boxes and cut a wavy line through the middle of each box on all four sides.

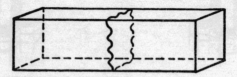

Separate the box into two parts by cutting on the wavy line with a razor knife. Cut off end flaps.

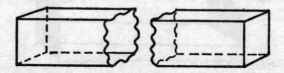

You now have two separate parts. Cut a straight line down one corner of each half.

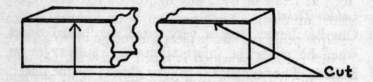

Unfold each half into a long strip.

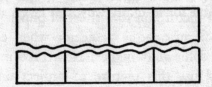

Lay the pieces next to one another, overlapping one on top of the other. Attach with staples and glue. Paint brown.

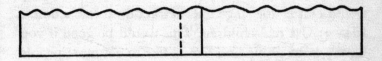

Chocolate River can be held at both ends and moved back and forth across the stage. It is now easy for Augustus Gloop to fall behind it and disappear in Scene 5.

Oompa-Loompas

Idea 1: On a flat piece of cardboard, sketch your own conception of an Oompa-Loompa. Cut it out and use it as a pattern to make others, and paint them all.

Idea 2: Draw or trace any figure you feel best represents an Oompa-Loompa. Put your picture on an opaque projector and project the image on to a piece of stiff cardboard which is taped to a wall. Go over the projected lines with a dark marker. Cut out and paint. Repeat process for exact replicas. If the projected image is not as large as you would like, project the original picture on to a sheet of paper (just small enough to fit in opaque projector when completed) to make it somewhat bigger. Now take marker and outline and use this picture to project on to cardboard.

Oompa-Loompas can be easily utilized in Scenes 5, 6 and 10, and can be propped up against anything. While they add colour and fun to your production, three to five are all that are necessary. Too many would clutter the stage and detract from the action.

Idea 3: Use real children. This would be good if you have a large group and would like to get more people involved.

Boat

Take one box at least 3 feet by 4 feet, and cut the top and bottom off.

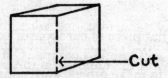

Cut one corner, and spread the box out flat.

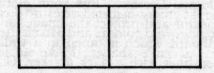

Draw boat on the box, as shown, and cut it out.

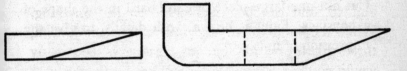

Take rectangular piece left over and make front to attach with staples and glue.

Paint the boat pink. Using staples and glue, put handles on the reverse (unpainted) side, using small pieces of cardboard.

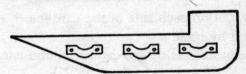

As the Chocolate River moves back and forth, the boat can slowly move from one side of the stage to the other, with Willy Wonka and the others behind it, holding it up with the handles on the back.

Secret Invention Room Machines
Get together as many assorted sizes of boxes as you want. Paint them wild colours and attach them to each other in any strange shapes. Make at least three

shapes or machines. Insert flashlights or blinking lights or anything that makes some sort of unusual noise into the boxes. One box should have a sign which reads, 'Great Gum Machine'.

Each machine can also have someone behind or inside it to vibrate it for added effect.

Pile of Nuts and Miniature Squirrels

Cut out one large piece of cardboard in the shape of a haystack. Paint it brown, with details, to give the impression of nuts.

Make a fold on each side of the cardboard, so that it will stand by itself.

Someone making noises and motions from behind the pile of nuts can suggest that the miniature squirrels are in the Nut Room.

Rubbish Chute

When Veruca Salt and her parents fall through the hole in the floor in Scene 8, they can 'fall' through a tunnel or long box with an opened end marked 'Garbage Chute'. Paint the box a dark colour.

Great Glass Elevator

In order to fit everyone inside, you should probably use two refrigerator boxes. Cut out one whole side of each box.

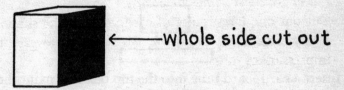

←——whole side cut out

Cut a doorway out of a second side of each box.

Put totally open sides together with both doorways facing out. Connect the two boxes with wire or fasteners.

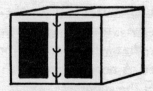

Paint and add glitter, coloured transparent paper, etc. The elevator can be moved about on stage if it is put on a moving platform or pushed. It can also be effective just to have someone behind it, shaking it gently. Lights flashing at this time will also give added effect.

TV Camera

This can be made simply by attaching several boxes together, one on top of the other.

Insert a cardboard tube into the top box and paint the whole thing black. Remember to check the balance of the boxes before attaching them to each other.

An Oompa-Loompa leaning against the camera can serve as the operator.

Chocolate Bar

Cut a big rectangle out of a piece of cardboard. Paint both sides with the name 'Willy Wonka'.

This is the bar that will disappear between the curtains in Scene 10. A normal-sized bar will reappear on the other side of the stage.

LIGHTING PROCEDURES

These procedures are practical if footlights, upper stage lights, and a spotlight are available. If you lack any of these, these suggestions will still help you get a general 'feel' for the desired effects. Remember that while your equipment may not be perfect, by using your imagination you can still provide atmosphere.

SCENE 1   *Spotlight* – on Narrator, then on four main characters as they are introduced
Footlights – red
Stage Uppers – red and blue

SCENE 2   *Spotlight* – off when Narrator has finished telling about family
Footlights – red
Stage Uppers – red and blue
LIGHTING CHANGE with action by Bucket family:
Footlights – add white to red
Stage Uppers – add white to red and blue

SCENE 3   *Spotlight* – off
Footlights – white and red
Stage Uppers – red and white and blue

SCENE 4   *Spotlight* – on Charlie and Grandpa Joe as they come up on one end of stage. Off as Charlie and Grandpa Joe join others in middle of stage
Footlights – red and white
Stage Uppers – blue

SCENE 5   *Spotlight* – off
Footlights – red and white
Stage Uppers – red and blue

SCENE 6   *Spotlight* – on as Narrator comes out to talk to audience. Off as Narrator leaves and boat approaches from other side
Footlights – red and blue
Stage Uppers – blue. Add white when Willy Wonka says 'Switch on the lights!'

SCENE 7   *Spotlight* – off
Footlights – red and blue. Red off at 'You're glowing!'
Stage Uppers – red. Red off and add Blue at 'You're glowing!'
LIGHTING CHANGE when Mrs Beauregarde and Veruca go off stage.
Footlights – add red to blue
Stage Uppers – take off blue and put on red

SCENE 8   *Spotlight* – off
Footlights – red and blue
Stage Uppers – red and white

SCENE 9 *Spotlight* – on Great Glass Elevator
Footlights – red and blue
Stage Uppers – red and white

SCENE 10 *Spotlight* – off
Footlights – red and blue
Stage Uppers – red and white and blue

SCENE 11 *Spotlight* – off
Footlights – red and blue
Stage Uppers – red and white and blue

ABOUT THE AUTHORS

Roald Dahl was born in 1916 in Wales of Norwegian parents. He was educated in England before starting work for the Shell Oil Company in Africa. He began writing after a 'monumental bash on the head' sustained as an RAF fighter pilot during the 2nd World War. Roald Dahl is one of the most successful and well-known of all children's writers. His books, which are read by children the world over, include *James and the Giant Peach*, *Charlie and the Chocolate Factory*, *The Magic Finger*, *Charlie and the Great Glass Elevator*, *Fantastic Mr Fox*, *The Twits*, *The BFG*, *The Witches*, winner of the 1983 Whitbread Award, and *Matilda*. Roald Dahl died in November 1990 at the age of seventy-four.

RICHARD R. GEORGE

Mr George has taught on the elementary school level in the USA for several years, producing a play a year. He originally adapted *Charlie and the Chocolate Factory* for his eleven-year-olds to perform and it was a great success. In addition to his teaching Mr George works with church and community youth groups. He was born in Buffalo, New York, and lives with his wife and their three children in Depew, New York.

ROALD DAHL'S FANTASTIC MR FOX: A PLAY
Adapted by Sally Reid

Now YOU can play a part in the exciting escapades of clever, handsome Fantastic Mr Fox and Boggis, Bunce and Bean, the nastiest farmers you've ever seen!

This excellent adaptation of Roald Dahl's popular story tell you everything you need to know to stage the play, and there are lots of parts for everyone – so get set for hours of fun!

ROALD DAHL'S THE BFG:
PLAYS FOR CHILDREN
Adapted by David Wood

Everybody loves the BFG. Now here's your chance to bring him to life! David Wood has created seven short plays for you to read and perform. With notes on simple staging, props and costumes, these plays can be produced with the minimum of experience and resources.

You'll have a phizzwizardly good time – and your friends won't be able to believe their gogglers!